THE
COLLABORATIVE
ARTIST

Silent Night

Franz Xaver Gruber

arranged by **Nancy Faber**

FLUTE PART

FABER
PIANO ADVENTURES

Silent Night

for Flute, Cello, and Piano

Franz Xaver Gruber
arranged by Nancy Faber

Flute

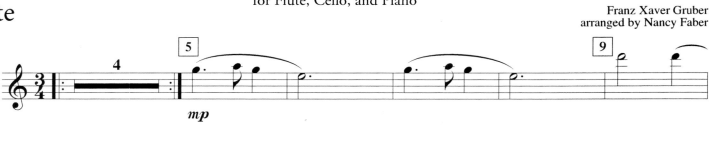
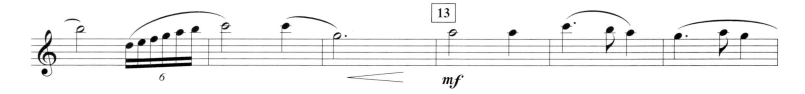

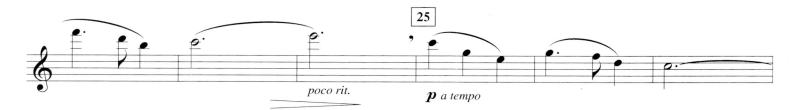
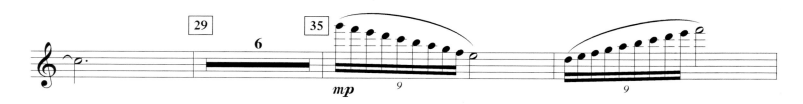
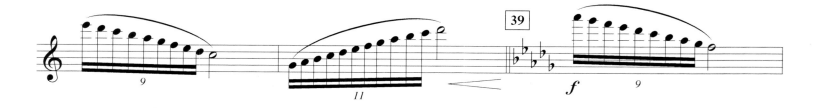
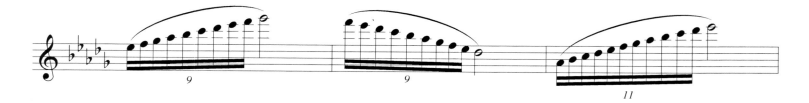

THE COLLABORATIVE ARTIST

Silent Night

Franz Xaver Gruber

arranged by **Nancy Faber**

CELLO PART

FABER

PIANO ADVENTURES®

Silent Night

for Flute, Cello, and Piano

Franz Xaver Gruber
arranged by Nancy Faber

Cello

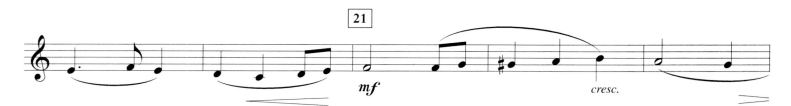

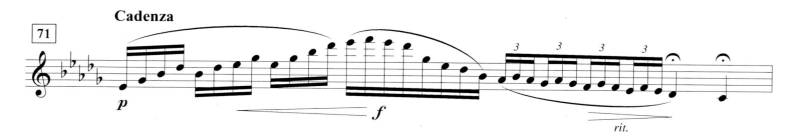

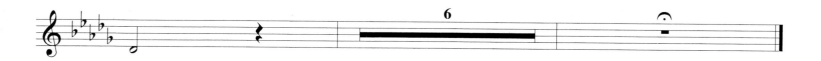

THE COLLABORATIVE ARTIST

Silent Night

for Flute, Cello, and Piano

Franz Xaver Gruber
arranged by Nancy Faber

ped. simile

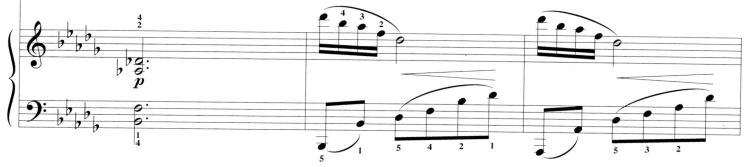

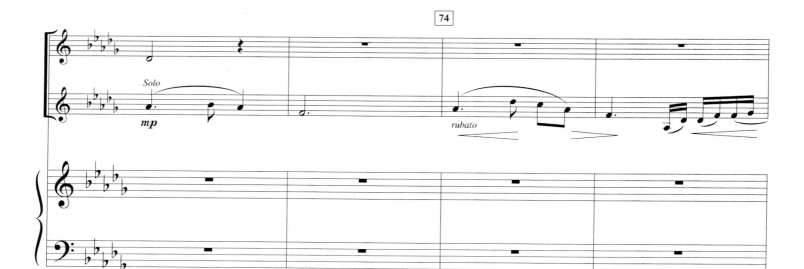